Queen Divas Body
SCULTING INC

BUSINESS EXPRESS MANUAL

SHARNELL B

TABLE OF CONTENTS

INTRODUCTION 1

1. QUICK BEGINNING STEPS 5

2. Q.D.B.S. LOGIC 10

3. YOU'RE IN 14

4. QUICK RESOURCES 16

5. FINALE 30

ACKNOWLEDGMENTS 33

Introduction

I have been wanting to do this business 6 - 7 years ago when I saw for the first time the Butt Enhancement Treatment about 6 years ago from Sculpting Goddess in Miami Florida on Instagram. I fell in love immediately.

Watching the process and then seeing the before and after results drove me wild. I knew one day I would travel to Florida to get one or two of her treatments but never thought she would end up being one of my Instructors. I wanted to do body sculpting years ago but because I am a Mom & Wife first I put my family first and did everything else except pursuing the body sculpting business. I knew in the back of my mind I would one day do it and now 6 - 7 years ago here i am. I moved away from NY to North Carolina for a year and a half. I had to come back to NY so I told my Husband I am coming back but i'm coming back with a vengeance. I am going to school to get the credentials I need to do body sculpting then once I graduate, get my own place and pursue what I've been wanting to do for years. I moved back to NY February 3, 2017, Started school February 6, 2017 and the rest is history. I started learning Ultrasound Cavitation & Skin tightening in NC so once I started school I bought my 1st Kim Slimming 8 5 in 1 Ultrasound Cavitation Machine and started practicing. I knew for me to get good I needed to start from somewhere so my husband and I set up an area in our home in the basement and "wallah" I started buying little things needed to start practicing on people so I bought my massage table, spa cart, Kim 8 Slimming machine, Ultrasound gel, towels, germicidal solution, cavi wipes, sheets, massage table warmer, disposable sheet covers, and all the other small items i needed, and lastly my first butt enhancement machine. So now I had my equipment and supplies to start my sister was my first client. My sister was my first model and first paying client. Once I started showing her results people were like Sha you are on to something so once others saw my sister results I got others that wanted my services and I just went full throttle. So while I'm doing my thing in my basement I started branching out bringing my machines to school and servicing my classmates on hands on days in school. I charged everyone $50 for any service. I tried the mobile business thing that was not my thing. It was too much lagging all the equipment plus the heavy massage table. I knew I had to work smarter not harder.

Realizing now I had a business that was on the rise and was in demand I needed more space. I needed to find a location, now I am looking around at office spaces and storefronts. So I started talking to my hubby and I was like I need to find a place. He said yes you do but do it the right way. He said do not rush into opening something until you speak to your teacher and hear what she tells you. He was like you still in school, you have no certificate or certification in what your doing, people love to sue out here just make ask her. My sister and I was at a place I liked way out in Long Beach Long island and was about to commit but something just didn't feel right. My husband said please call her now. So that's what i dd. I never listened to anyone but I really admired my teacher and believed that whatever advice she gave me it will be genuine. I called her she told me just wait. She said people love to sue and God forbid if anything happens you do not want to jeopardize your license for in the near future. So i just kept perfecting my craft in June flew to Miami, Florida and took class with the Sculpting Goddess. She taught me a lot and refreshed what I already did.

Very informative, great instructor and it was worth the trip. The class i took I did butt enhancement, butt lift, cellulite treatments grade 1,2, & 3, Breast lift, shock wave therapy - (EMS), Cavitation, Laser lipo, skin tightening, and wood therapy. So with all that I learned plus what i knew I was ready for the world. I paused on looking for places and just focused on school and looking to graduate. In August 2017 I graduated. I immediately scheduled my state board test. I passed on the 1st go round which was God's blessing. I then started looking again for places to open. It was hard and even very discouraging at times even when I was looking and in school it's not easy looking for the ideal place to open for the first time. As i looked I needed a few more machines and reached out to some of the popular Instagrammers that do body sculpting on where I could purchase the machines I was missing. NO ONE WANTS TO HELP!

People rather charge you and charge you double and triple for the same machines you can get on you own. I never gave up. I kept researching and did not give up until I found what i was looking for. By the grace of God everything came together for me even when I thought about giving up because of the opposition, stress, and discouragement at times. I did my research once I did open. I had my license, business license, all the equipment I needed and the rest is history. Always believe in you, you will never go wrong. I opened my first office in Elmont for my 1st year. I did not renew my lease there, found a bigger and better place that's now in Franklin Square, NY. I am so grateful and thankful. If something is your calling God will open the doors for you no matter what the opposition is and let's add the Naysayers to. This is the introduction to how I got started personally and wanted to say you can do it!!!

1

QUICK BEGINNING STEPS

The basic beginning steps you will need to get started. Before I list the steps first and foremost have CPA - Certified Public Accountant. Let them help you with the right steps to follow. Get a good one though. I have one if you need it!

#1 - First and foremost when you're looking for a space the cardinal rule is Location, Location, Location. Make sure you research your demographics for where you are trying to open. Make sure your business fits in the area and check your competition if any. I looked in area where there was no competition. If there is none take advantage and push your brand. Make sure if your signing a lease it all makes sense. Try to do a one year lease and not let anyone lock you into a 3 or 5 year lease. Anything can happen in life and God forbid if you have to close down your now stuck in a 3 or 5 year lease. These landlords want money. Be smart.

#2 - Once you found your location you must acquire your business license. Research your county or city to find the business license office. Once you get your license you are ready to go. Always make sure your Business License is always visible with your professional license whether its Esthetics, cosmetology, or massage therapist. Make sure its visible.

#3 - Hiring. Of course we know hiring is not an easy transition. If you are going to hire people immediately screen people well. You are giving people keys to your space your dream do a background check. First think of people you know that can use a job. If you can keep it close sometimes that is better than a stranger but it can also smack you in the behind because people fill you know them they have favoritism so they are or become lazy. Do not let anyone run your business in the ground. Separate business from personal. That's how I am. I can love you to death but I will fire you without a blink. For hiring you can put an ad in the newspaper, instagram, facebook, Craigslist, set up an account with Indeed, zip recruiter, and you can ask people if people know reliable and trustworthy people. Be creative in how you want to hire individuals.

#4 - Marketing & Advertising. Once you got your space and signed your lease start marketing your business as soon as possible. The more you get your business out the better. The more money you spend on marketing the better your results are. It's people that spend thousands monthly on marketing & advertising. Do what you can afford. Stay in your lane. If you have it beautiful if not it will come. You don't have to spend thousands in the beginning to get clients. I use a mixture. I market and advertise with Yelp, Google Ads, Instagram, Facebook campaigns, Web.com, Groupon, Chamber of Commerce, USPS direct marketing, passing out flyers, mouth to mouth, referral program, Square Campaigns, etc. Find your own groove and go with what you feel will work for you and your business. Again Be creative. (Groupon has its Pros and Cons. You get paid twice a month and it is best to get a Representative I will list mines later)

#5 - Your setup cleaning, decor, organizing documents, organize your theme rooms, setting up all your equipment, hanging all your licenses, certificates, and certifications. Set your space up for you and what you feel is suitable for your clients. Clients love a clean, great smelling, well decorated space. You should be now getting ready to open the door.

If you're planning a Grand Opening be creative with the price of services, gifts, refreshments, and decorations. I have not yet done my Re Grand opening. It's all on you and how you want to run your business. I did not do a business plan that would be the first step if you choose to go that route. I been wanting to do this for so long that I already had my plan together and I executed it the way that worked for me. You have to make it work for you. If you feel setting up a business plan is key for you then please do that. If your going through a franchise everything is setup for you so it is not as much to worry about. Independent is a lot more to do because your on your own unless you have a partner. As you get into the groove of what you are trying to accomplish. There are many books to follow and read but you must find your own way. Do not depend on what others portray on social media or get into too much popularity. Everyone's journey is different. Never compare yourself to anyone and always remember nothing will just come easy. It took some people years to get to where they are today. If someone had an overnight success story God Bless them but most go through the trials and tribulations. The 1st year to 2nd Year of business are the hardest but if you can get through year 1 on your way to the 2nd year should be a little bit easier. Nothing is promised to any of us but as long as you're not hesitant, but consistent and persistent you will be fine. You have to go out on a Leap of Faith and know God has you no matter what. Once you love what you do and are passionate half the battle is over. Loving what you do is the key!

Our businesses is not only what you want to set you up for the rest of your life it is also a number game. A number game that must always be in control so you can have longevity. I will go more into that a little later.

2

Q.D.B.S. LOGIC

I can go on and on with what you can and what you should not do with a business but actual proof and putting the work in is the proof. Everyone's business is different. You want to be different from others no matter how small it maybe offer something to your clients others do not do. Always make sure your clients are happy and they receive outstanding service all across the board.

Now when I said before about your business being a numbers game I meant that. You must track and calculate every expense. That means rent, light bill, possibly water bill, cable, trash pick up, insurance, payroll, supplies, and marketing / advertising monthly. These are recurring expenses. You must include everything monthly so you can gauge how much you should be making monthly. You gauge it daily, weekly, bi weekly, or monthly. Always look to make double or triple your expenses. So let's do numbers. If your expenses are $5,000 in total you need to be bringing in 2x to 3x that to sustain. So If your spending $5,000 you should be making $10,000 - $15,000 monthly. You may say how do I do this. Be marketable. Have many different ways of bringing in income under the same roof.

So if you have to be a one stop shop then that is what you need to do. Make it easier for your clients as well so they do not have to figure out where else they need to go for other services. So if your a hair salon do hair, make up, eyelash extensions, facials, waxing, and resell products.

Have more than hair. So if hair slows down you have the eyelash extensions, or waxing, etc. Always capital the market. Cover everything. Look into trademark, patenting, Corporating and copyrights. Brand yourself not only by marketing but by owning your brand. Keeping it off limits to others that would like to steal your brand.

If they did infringe on your business name you can take them to court and sue them. None of these methods are free but make your business name matter. CPA. Make sure you have an accountant. You must pay business taxes quarterly that's every 3 months. Make sure your accountant is doing what he or she is supposed to do. You do not want any issues with the IRS. There are programs you can use like Quickbooks. Quickbooks can do everything for you even payroll. You pay for different services with QB. I started out with Groupon as a tool for clients. As I went along I got referrals then I started with yelp and other methods of bringing in customers. There is no right and wrong when it comes to how you market and advertise. Whatever works for you that is what you do. This is a guide and just advice from what I do. If you choose to follow that is solely up to you but I put it out there you can incorporate what you choose to get the results you get. I worked by appointment only. I like organization. I do not want my place to be in anarchy by having walk ins on top of booked appointments. Again I work alone the having employees did not work for me but I like appointment only. If you have a full team and you want to do walk ins and appointments knock yourself out. I like the organization of everyone coming in at a time and I finish by a certain time. I like to work smarter not harder. I hope to find an outstanding team, I know i will i am picky and you should be picky to once your business is on the line. It only takes 1 person to tarnish your brand. So always make sure your on your employees, have meetings weekly or bi weekly, and do evaluations. You want the best with you, the cream of the crop. It is nothing wrong with demanding the best.

3

❦

YOU'RE IN

So now you're in the space you've chose and it feels so good and you feel free and elated. Now comes the hard work. You should be setting up your appointments, booking clients, servicing your clients, and doing the same thing each and everyday whether you work 5, 6, 0r 7 days a week. Make sure you stay on your employees.

Make sure they are giving the clients outstanding customer service skills. That goes along way in business. Word of mouth is huge and referrals. It can make you and break you. Always stand out! Remember you want to be making 2 - 3 x the amount you spend out. Regardless you always want to double and triple your revenue. Will you make profits the 1st year possibly or you may break even then the 2nd year you will make a profit. It is your business so matter how you slice the pie you are looking to make money. Nothing is overnight so you must be patient. As long as you put the work in, you will get the rewards. If you open a business and you make lots of money the 1st year that's a blessing. Always know you can and you will achieve greatness. Stay organized, get a booking site, Take deposits, remember time is money money is time, set up a merchant account where you can take debit and credit cards. If you choose to do payment plans it's up to you, I don't. I use to but you end up getting burnt so I do not. Be willing to do consultations whether free or you charge. Clients do not liked to be rushed. I personally do not do free consultations. Have a website set up. Also do some type of reward system for clients. Mines is refer 3 people get a free service. Those 3 people must buy services and commit for the client to get the free client and I have exclusions. You can do buy 10 get 1 free or 2 people get a service the 3rd person get theirs free or half off. Don't be afraid to try different things in your business to help it grow. It's time for YOU to shine and Queen Divas Body Sculpting is praying for you and know you can achieve anything you put your mind to.

4

QUICK RESOURCES

This is just a few websites and people you can reach out to for help and or services. Don't be afraid to research that's what I did. No one helped me I had to do it alone so don't be afraid to fail in research. I did but got it together.

Business License:

<u>Brooklyn</u>
Kings County Clerk's Office

Supreme Court Building 360 Adams Street

Room 189

Brooklyn, NY 11201

Phone: (347) 404-9750

Website:

http://www.nycourts.gov/courts/2jd/kingsclerk/index.shtml

Bronx

Bronx County Clerk's Office

851 Grand Concourse

Room 118

Bronx, NY 10451

Phone: (866) 797-7214

Fax: (718) 590-8122

Website: http://bronxcountyclerkinfo.com/

Manhattan

New York County Clerk's Office

60 Centre Street

Room 161

New York , NY 10007 Phone: (646) 386-5955

Website:

http://www.nycourts.gov/courts/1jd/supctmanh/county_clerk_operations.shtml

BUSINESS EXPRESS MANUAL

Queens

Queens County Clerk's Office

88-11 Sutphin Boulevard 1st Floor

Jamaica, NY 11435

Phone: (718) 298-0605

Website:

http://www.nycourts.gov/COURTS/11jd/queensclerk/index.shtml

Staten Island

Richmond County Clerk's Office

130 Stuyvesant Place

2nd Floor Staten Island, NY 10301

Phone: (718) 675-7700

Website: http://www.richmondcountyclerk.com/

NYS Division of Licensing Services

Website: www.Dos.ny.gov

Esthetics

The practice of "esthetics" means providing for a fee, or any consideration or exchange, whether direct or indirect, services to enhance the appearance of the face, neck, arms, legs, and shoulders of a human being by the use of compounds or procedures including makeup, eyelashes, depilatories, tonics, lotions, waxes, sanding and tweezing, whether performed by manual, mechanical, chemical or electrical means and instruments but shall not include the practice of electrology. *It is the responsibility of licensees to understand the Appearance Enhancement Law*. (pdf)

Cosmetology

The practice of "cosmetology" means providing service to the hair, head, face, neck or scalp of a human being, including but not limited to shaving, trimming, and cutting the hair or beard either by hand or mechanical appliances and the application of antiseptics, powders, oils, clays, lotions or applying tonics to the hair, head, or scalp, and in addition includes providing, for a fee or any consideration or exchange, whether direct or indirect, services for the application of dyes, reactive chemicals, or other preparations to alter the color or to straighten, curl, or alter the structure of the hair of a human being. *It is the responsibility of licensees to understand the Appearance Enhancement Law*.

Nail Specialty

The practice of "nail specialty" means providing services for a fee or any consideration or exchange to cut, shape or to enhance the appearance of the nails of the hands or feet. Nail specialty includes the application and removal of sculptured or artificial nails. *It is the responsibility of licensees to understand the Appearance Enhancement Law*. (pdf)

Notice to All Nail Salon Business Owners

The New York Department of State ("Department") has created several new handouts and educational materials concerning new rules relating to ventilation. If your business offers nail specialty services, the Department advises you to review these materials and contact us if you have any questions. All materials are available below.

To help your business comply with the new regulations, the Department has created:
- General Guidance - Overview of the New Regulations
- The Business Owner's How to Guide to Ventilation
- Important Tips & Information After an Inspection
- Technical Specifications for Contractors and Professionals
- Useful Resources Guide and Helpful Links
- FAQs Relating to Ventilation

For additional information about the rule, please visit:
http://www.dos.ny.gov/licensing/appearance/ventingreg.html

THE BUSINESS OWNER'S GUIDE HOW TO GUIDE TO VENTILATION

(English) (Spanish/Español) (Haitian-Creole/Kreyòl Ayisyen)

(Italian/Italiano) (Korean/한국어) (Russian/Русский)

(Chinese/中文) (Vietnamese/Việt) (Nepali/नेपाल1) (Tibetan/ བོད་སྐད་)

NAIL SPECIALTY VENTILATION IMPORTANT TIPS & INFORMATION AFTER AN INSPECTION

(English) (Spanish/Español) (Haitian-Creole/Kreyòl Ayisyen)

(Italian/Italiano) (Korean/한국어) (Russian/Русский)

(Chinese/ 中 文) (Vietnamese/Việt) (Nepali/नेपाल1) (Tibetan/ བོད་སྐད་)

TECHNICAL SPECIFICATIONS FOR CONTRACTORS AND PROFESSIONALS

(English) (Spanish/Español) (Haitian-Creole/Kreyòl Ayisyen)

(Italian/Italiano) (Korean/한국어) (Russian/Русский)

(Chinese/中文) (Vietnamese/Việt) (Nepali/नेपाल1) (Tibetan/ བོད་སྐད་)

VENTILATION CERTIFICATION

(English) (Spanish/Español) (Haitian-Creole/Kreyòl Ayisyen)

(Italian/Italiano) (Korean/한국어) (Russian/Русский)

(Chinese/中文) (Vietnamese/Việt) (Nepali/नेपाल1) (Tibetan/ བོད་སྐད་)

BUSINESS EXPRESS MANUAL

THE SAME INFORMATION GOES TO RESIDENTS UPSTATE NEW YORK

Natural Hair Styling

The practice of "natural hair styling" means providing for a fee, or any consideration or exchange, whether direct or indirect, any of the following services to the hair of a human being: shampooing, arranging, dressing, twisting, wrapping, weaving, extending, locking or braiding the hair or beard by either hand or mechanical appliances. Such practice shall not include cutting, shaving or trimming hair except that such activities are permissible to the extent that such activities are incidental to the practice of natural hair styling. Such practice shall not include the application of dyes, reactive chemicals, or other preparations to alter the color or to straighten, curl, or alter the structure of the hair. Techniques which result in tension on hair roots such as certain types of braiding, weaving, wrapping, locking and extending of the hair may only be performed by a natural hair styling or cosmetology licensee who has successfully completed an approved course of study in such techniques. *It is the responsibility of licensees to understand the Appearance Enhancement Law*. (pdf)

Waxing

The practice of "natural hair styling" means providing for a fee, or any consideration or exchange, whether direct or indirect, any of the

22

following services to the hair of a human being: shampooing, arranging, dressing, twisting, wrapping, weaving, extending, locking or braiding the hair or beard by either hand or mechanical appliances. Such practice shall not include cutting, shaving or trimming hair except that such activities are permissible to the extent that such activities are incidental to the practice of natural hair styling. Such practice shall not include the application of dyes, reactive chemicals, or other preparations to alter the color or to straighten, curl, or alter the structure of the hair. Techniques which result in tension on hair roots such as certain types of braiding, weaving, wrapping, locking and extending of the hair may only be performed by a natural hair styling or cosmetology licensee who has successfully completed an approved course of study in such techniques. *It is the responsibility of licensees to understand the Appearance Enhancement Law*. (pdf)

Groupon Merchant Representative

Ryan Plunkett

Merchant Development Rep. | GROUPON

Phone 773-696-4241

rplunkett@groupon.com

Support: merchantsupport@groupon.com

BUSINESS EXPRESS MANUAL

YELP

Website: www.biz.yelp.com

YELP REPRESENTATIVE

Chloe Castillo | Account Executive, Yelp Inc. P: 312-429-5196

Email: chloec@yelp.com

CPA - Accountant / Finance

Steve Hartman - (516) 457 - 8252

Allisha Settles - (347) 515 -8825

Website: allishaporter.wixsite.com/

IG: jlsettlesbookkeeping

Merchant Services

Any bank Preferably your personal bank - TD Bank, Chase, Citi Bank, etc.

www.Squareup.com

www.paypal.com

www.shopkeep.com

www.paymentcloud.com

Website Builders

www.wix.com

www.sitebuilder.com

www.weebly.com

www.shopify.com

Booking / Appointment Sites

www.booksy.com

www.simplybook.me/en

www.sqaureup.com

www.wix.com

www.glossgenius.com

www.clickbook.net

www.setmore.com

PAYROLL

Quickbooks

Quickbooks.intuit.com

ADP

Adp.com

Gusto

go.gusto.com/small_business/payroll

BUSINESS EXPRESS MANUAL

Paychex

www.paychex.com

SquareUp Payroll

www.squareup.com

Esthetics / Body Sculpting - Equipment

www.spaelf.com

www.Bellaskinusa.com

www.massagewarehouse.com

www.purespadirect.com www.spasupplies.com

www.Copasdelfin.com

www.advance-esthetic.us/vacuum-machine-for-buttocks - *Their very expensive*

www.topspasupply.com

www.buyritebeauty.com

www.cosmoprofbeauty.com

www.ebay.com

www.amazon.com

WhatsApp

Skin Dermotherapies +57 316 7380122 - Butt Machine / Breast Cups - use Queen Divas Body Sculpting you will get a discount

Disenos D Prada Fajas

+1 (401) 543-8733

Delfin Copas - Butt Machine

+57 316 3977101

TRAINING

Body Sculpting / Body Contouring Training

Queen Divas Body Sculpting

1040 Hempstead Turnpike

Suite LL1

Franklin Square, NY 11010

www.queendivasbodysculpting.com

queendivasbodysculpting@gmail.com

(347) 433 - 5580

Sculpting Goddess

190 NE 199th Street Suite 201

Miami, Florida 33179

www.sculptinggoddess.com

info@sculptinggoddess.com

(786) 245 - 9598

Locations: Miami, Lake Worth, Tallahassee, California, Las Vegas - Coming Soon

BUSINESS EXPRESS MANUAL

Eyelash Extension Training

Royalty Lash Bar

315 Walt Whitman Rd Huntington Station, NY 11746

www.royaltylashbar.com

book@royaltylashbar.com

(844) 888 - 5274

Eyelash Extension Co.

204 Pacific Coast Hwy

Suite 211

Lomita, CA 90713

Pretty Lashes LA

mcclairenterprise@gmail.com

(310) 424 - 8217

Frontal Lace Training

Tatianna

IG: tati_didit

stylesbytati.as.me/ Miami, Fl

(347) 968 - 4527

Also sells Bundles

Does Makeup & Eyelash Extensions

Continued on Training - This is just a few individuals that are licensed and have experience in what they do for training. Always go for good trainers. Do not get caught up in Popularity, you may be disappointed. I get DM's on people that have taken training with popular individuals and were not happy and spent lots of money for training. I will say this over and over, research, research, research It helped me. Again this is just express information to help your transition easy. If I forgot anyone that's a trainer sorry these are people that are close to me and I believe and Know the skill level. You won't be unhappy. Always be willing to promote others and help them if you can. We have to change the world one day at a time with positivity and spreading love.

Lastly Every State is different with rules for licensing so please research and make sure you know what the law is for getting your professional license and business license.

5

FINALE

I hope this Express Manual was very helpful in your start or even just the thought of being an entrepreneur. It is definitely not easy but it is rewarding. I tell people all the time there is no getting rich with a 9 to 5 and it's the God's honest truth. I rather slay for myself and be good than to be a slave for someone that does not appreciate me. I set the tone for my business.

I have the flexibility of whatever my schedule needs to be, try that with a 9 to 5 and see where you will be. I did not get into numbers as far as my business goes because number one i am a straight forward person with no gimmicks and lies, the second thing is everybody's business is different if i make $20,000 a month does not mean you will so i try to stay away from the shaded areas with numbers. Q.D.B.S is good. I am still standing being able to write this Ebook and letting you know some of the Pros and Cons with business. My doors are still opened and I am always looking to add services to the business. I feel like I have accomplished a lot in year by myself with no partner so I must give praises to myself. I started just like some of you reading this book with no help and no one wanting to give me some of the information I put in this book. People wanted to charge me. To each thine own. Somethings yes I can see you asking money for but equipment that is public record to me that is just sad. That is why I researched for hours days losing sleep to get all I needed to get before I graduated from Esthetics school. I hope I am the breath of fresh air for some of you starting. I've gotten enough DM's on the same issue of people not answering back or them charging people for knowing equipment. I want this to be an easy transition. It is not the end all but it is a good start for you to get to where you need to be. I love helping people as long as you are not trying to take advantage of the situation. We are all teachers in our own ways. We can never stop learning. I tried to cover the most basic steps needed in this book.

Research, research, research, research. This is the answer too so many questions. I did it so can you. Lastly I want to say about

BUSINESS EXPRESS MANUAL

training. If you are looking for training research. Don't just go on social media see the most popular people that train and think that is the end all because it's not. Always remember the smallest lion roars louder than a bigger popular Lion. Popularity is not everything.

Thanks to you all I appreciate you all that support and use this book for yourself and others. I am so appreciative you have no idea how appreciative and humble i am. Again I want you all to shine, shine brighter than the sun. You can and You will. QDBS Deems it in Jesus name.

Kisses
xoxoxo

Acknowledgments

I would like to thank my kids. They are my biggest cheerleaders. Tatianna my oldest baby you helped push me emotionally when I was ready to give up in the beginning the words at the time a 24 year old spoke were like an old man's tale and proverbs. I thank you so much for those words and seeing my vision exactly how I saw it. I love you and thank you so much. Tahirah my 11 year old baby. You stick to your mother no matter what and I mean that literally you are with me almost 90% of time.

You tell me how much you love me, you hug me, you tell me I'm beautiful, I'm the best mom in the world and no one is like me. Your my receptionist at the office, you make my clients sign in you are best 11 year old in the world. I am glad I'm your mom and I love you soooooo much and I will always be here for you. To my mother

BUSINESS EXPRESS MANUAL

Lillie your like me to the point and straight forward. I thank you for believing in me to. I love you so much and I thank you for being the mom you are. To my sister Michelle. I thank you for believing in me and being my very 1st client. LOL. You to cheered me on when I was ready to throw in the towel early in my quest. You told me the words I needed to dust myself off and get right back at it. You said to me "I can't believe you ready to quit when you have a gift. You touch people one time and give them the best results and you trying to quit, that's not my sister." I needed to hear all that you said. I get and got it. I love you to. To everyone else close to me and not close to me that cheered me on and believe in me I thank you and appreciate you. Also my clients I thank you and appreciate you supporting QDBS and I could not have done it with you ladies & gents. Last but not least my rock and my love my husband Lenny. You are my partner, my other half, my friend, and most of all the love of my life. We been through so much. Started from the bottom now we here. You with your successful company cheering me on telling me how proud you are means and meant so much to me. You have my back no matter what. I thank you from the bottom of my heart for being here and loving me the way you do. I love you so much and thank you for dealing with my QDBS craziness all the time.

Thank you God I could not do anything without you. You opened each door for me seamlessly with no hems. Yes I wanted to give up when things went to the left but you didn't let that happen.

You kept me in the fight. You made every transaction check out with no more hiccups. I love you pass the moon in Jesus name. Without you there's no us. Jesus you know my heart, you know me. I love you, I love you, I love you.

Sharnell B
Owner of Queen Divas Body Sculpting Inc.

www.ingramcontent.com/pod-product-compliance
Lightning Source LLC
Chambersburg PA
CBHW031506210526
45463CB00003B/1100